BLACKM

BLACK MAN WHERE IS YOUR GOD

What can I say but how precious?
How precious it is to be **BLACK AND PROUD**
Educated
Family oriented
Blessed
God given
Racist
Heavenly

Yes you will fume at racist, but racist is not based on racial
hatred but true love for the different races – faces
*YES THE TRUE BLACK RACE.*

Mother and Father are we
We gave birth to child - children
The universe
Different kingdoms

We are special, hence the truth that resides in us
Our spirituality
Universal right
Truths

Michelle Jean

Wow because life is so weird, hence I ask, Black Man where is your God?

It seems the more educated we become in the Babylonian system of things is the stupider we get. No sorry, the more inept and illiterate we become; are.

We've become arrogant, self centered and self absorbed that it is beyond me how some of you can't smell your own stench (shit) literally.

*To you the black race, no black man that say inorganic foods are superior to organic foods; know this, inorganic foods will never be superior to organic foods no matter the soil content. We humans are the ones to pollute the soil content of earth with the chemicals we produce. Chemicals that are airborne – rise up and take shape in the triosphere. And yes this is my version of earth's life taken into account the biological composition (biosphere, human evolution and spiritual development – beginning and end). Yes life and death. We have to factor in the spiritual realm into the equation because life on earth do affect and alter spiritual life in some way; whether that way be positive or negative. Life isn't determined by organic matter – foods such as fruits, food from the ground. Life is dependent and determined on water in both worlds. Water is the determining factor in life hence water is found abundantly on earth and in the realm of life. But water cannot be found in hell. Hell is the house of fire hence you have the houses of fire (ministries and so much more on earth today).*

*As humans we want to become the creator and or creators but can't create a damned thing a part from mess and stress; heartache and pain.*

So this book goes out to the black educated fools that think they are so educated that they are higher and better than the normal black man or woman. You are not better than me or the next man and or person; woman. You are just another token black that is in the economy; grand scheme of slavery, the devil's evil system of things. Until you have something for yourself then you are no better than me. All you are telling me is that you graduated from Massa's fields. Now it's your turn to deceive and manipulate your own with the lies Massa told you and gave to you to feed and fool your own. You're not free. You're still a slave with a slave mentality. Hence you are bred – educated and well versed in books of slavery – bondage.

You now have to capture your own and sell them the bullshit Massa instilled in you. Your education is that of slaves – slave taught, hence you're still Massa's bitch because at the end of the day, you still have to answer to Massa; kiss his White and Black ass. You still have to give account to Massa; give him and or her their due; pay. You're not free. You're controlled, his puppet because you cannot cut the strings of him; her.

*Know this, GOD – GOOD GOD AND ALLELUJAH GAVE US ALL ORGANIC EVERYTHING. MAN IS THE ONE TO POLLUTE SOIL AND AIR INCLUDING WATER TO MAKE US GET SICK SO THAT WE HAVE TO BUY THEIR CRAP – SO CALLED MEDICINES; CHEMICALLY INDUCED FOODS.* We pay for death hence medicines; modern day medicines are not designed to cure, they were designed to kill; take human life at will. Your so called medicines kill our internal organs hence all that you say these medicines do do not profit the human population on a whole, they profit the Pharmaceutical Companies and Morgues – Dead Houses globally. We've become controlled beings that have been led on death's road for centuries by the system – Babylonian System of Control, Dominance, Man and Death.

Irregardless of the earth's soil content, all within earth is organic because the chemicals of man can only reach so far in the soil. Hence chemicals are surface agents and surface agents only. So to say nothing is organic is false. Remember, plants and trees do not change their soil content; man did with the pollution we introduced into the soil and the chemicals we emit into the air. So truly think because in all we do, we are truly wrong, truly don't care.

**_The water that comes down via rainfall cleans the earth of its pollutants. The trees clean the air of its pollutants but there is only so much the trees and rain can do to help man – humanity. We are the dirty ones because we dirty Earth not Earth dirty self. We are the nasty ones that truly cannot clean; clean our mess and messes we made in her (Earth)._**

Yes earth is losing the battle due to man's evils. So when any of you say chemically induced medicines and foods are better than what he Good God and Allelujah has and have given us, I say to you, truly go fuck yourselves. You go against God hence you are truly not needed here on Earth in Good God's kingdom. Stay in the devil's kingdom and domain (land and lands) because you are truly of the devil and not Good God's own. You side with evil against Good God hence you serve no purpose – good purpose when it comes to good and true live. You side with evil to destroy Earth hence Earth must do her duty and truly leave you alone to the evil and evils you choose for her – chemical gain; death of soil and soil content of the earth.

Nothing is better than what he Good God and Allelujah has and have given us. Duly note and remember, the polluted earth is where you get the herbs and plants you need to produce the crap that you call medicines that you give to man – humanity to help them; so called save them. But in fact all you give to humanity sends us and or them to an early grave. Yes this is your population control hence Earth must rebel real soon.

Man did not create the trees Good God did. So if you are against him Good God and Allelujah, why the fuck are you still on Earth? Why are you using his trees and bushes; herbs to make your medicines? Should you not be making your own from the thin air? No you can't use the air nor should you be able to and or allowed to use the natural chemicals of the earth to produce your own. All is polluted so truly do not use anything Good God and Allelujah own including all that is Earth owned. Come on now.

***If your chemically induced shit is so superior to organic, why are there so many deaths, birth defects, medical complications+ associated to the crap that you produce and sell to us and feed us? Truly don't use any of God's –***

*<u>Good God and Allelujah's supplies if organic is so bad. Find another universe. No create your own damned inorganic universe and go there to live come on now. No, go to your universe that you create for self and stay the hell away from God's – Good God's stuff. No bones are provided for you anymore so get the hell lost and don't touch Good God's stuff. Come on now. You don't care for him and you put down his things so get your own by your own damned means. Damn bare face and bright. Outtaada and wrenk; stink.</u>*

*KNOW THIS, MONEY DOES NOT OUTWEIGH LIFE, LIFE OUTWEIGHS MONEY BECAUSE WHEN YOU ARE DEAD AND GONE MOTHER EARTH WILL STILL BE HERE. All the inorganic crap (things) you plant must die and will die along with you so that Earth, Mother Earth can truly replenish self and clean self.*

*Life isn't about conquest and lies. Hence I ask you the educated BLACK FOOLS, WHAT MAKES YOU EDUCATED AND VERSED WHEN IT COMES TO LIFE when you know not a damned thing about life and how life started; came into being? Many of you work for others and not self. You can't even build your own nations because you're all dependent on others for a damned hand out – monetary bail out; funds (IMF). Our nations are barren and down trodden hence the burdens of many Black Lands. Black Lands we refuse to build positively and prosperously but yet many of you have the gaul to talk. Talk as if you know. You're all had hence the system sleeps with many of you and kill hundreds of millions of you. Africa, ah the beauty of Africa. Africa is life because without Africa all would die. Every life whether human, spiritual, organic, (plant, trees, water and air) you name would die.*

*Why the hell do you think the devil is trying so hard to make Africa and Africans barren, destitute, disease ridden; plagued – dead? Black People you had better wake up because the devil knows life must go back to Africa and begin again. Hence he's doing all to keep life – true life out of Africa indefinitely.*

*Black Man, Woman and Child wake up because the Exodus begins and it starts with us; every Black Man, Woman and Child.*

Let me ask you this. Is it the lies you're brainwashed in in BABYLONIAN SOCIETIES OF LIES that makes you intellectual? Or is it the arrogance associated with you and is engrained in you? Hence Bob Marley said it best. "The Babylon System is a Vampire sucking the children day by day." Hence the Pagan System (Babylonian System) is sucking you and draining you of everything including your own spirit and soul – life.

It's amazing how we turn coat and abandon Good God for the Babylonian Way then have the audacity to think God – Good God is with any of us. Come on now.

Tell me something, WHAT GOOD IS EDUCATION IF THERE IS NO TRUTH BEHIND IT?

***Many of you were taught lies hence your ignorance in all that you do is worth naught in the end. Know this, it's all your so called intelligence that has and have destroyed earth. Your so called intelligence that have and has put billions in the extinction line of death literally.***

And don't you dare say we're not on the extinction line because we are technologically advanced. We can avert any destruction. We have satellites that can and will give us the heads up when it comes to destruction. Bullshit because humanity isn't technologically advanced. You are just catching up to that point in time for your little piece of discovery. What you know now and or is discovering now was set in time at a point in time long ago. You are just catching up to that time and technology. And with all that said your technology is inferior to that of other universes. The technology of these universes is way more advanced hence our minds cannot correlate time. Nor can we properly measure and or tell time; a distance in time. Things have to be given to us in bits and pieces because we lack education, intellectual skills; knowledge. Wow if only you knew the advancement of technology that is on the moon. You know not time or space travel hence space travel is just a thought and not a reality for man. You can only think of what other planets look like but cannot step foot on them hence you lie about man walking on the moon. If man walked on the moon then they would have found an advanced race people that can travel through time; space just like that. There are no alien races as scientists would have us believe. The race of the moon looks exactly like me and you; fleshy beings in time; space. And it's not dough the space station is there. Going to the space station is not space travel because man cannot travel to the real moon nor can they travel to other planets to steal their advanced technology. Your moon is pure ice because it cools the earth down and man; humanity have not the technology to travel there. If they did, they would know the opening in time and they would know the time in time. They would reach that point in time when they are self reliant and independent of physical time; food but not water. We think in the physical hence we know not the spiritual nor can we conceive and comprehend the spiritual. If we did, Earth would be void of war and strife; hatred hence the alternate universe we are in. This is our bubble; physical hell. And this is not for you to comprehend because the life you're living is already lived hence from time to time you will feel as if you were in this place already, meaning already lived this life. Your life is like a sleeping state hence the dreams of man. Dream inna dream that many of us have and has.

There is another world that houses real life but getting there all depends on the life you live on earth. Hence there is a heaven and hell as you call them – these worlds. Yes the moon can be deadly but death has his own planet for which I call the moon but in truth it's not the moon. It's another distant planet that house evil spirits. Spirits we call demons that come to earth to wreak havoc in some of our lives. And I am going to leave things at this because you're all thinking I am crazy and need to be in the loony bin. But as humans what you cannot conceive you say it's nonexistent; not real when in fact it is real. You know not this world and time hence you cannot conceive it; know it. You know not the planet of death hence death come to man and not life. Death takes your life because of sin; your sins.

We are still primitive hence you know not to kill. We kill each other like savages and say we are civilized when we are not. Hence we prey on the dead and eat the carcass of the dead.

No, I am bent. We as blacks parade around and pree Babylon but yet truly do not know that Babylon hates our asses. We do not know that He (Satan) would do anything to wipe us off the face of the planet. Hence Babylon steal our history, heritage and culture whist having you admiring and basking in their filth.

**_Bob Marley told us in his song, Babylon System but like he said, "we are too ignorant to know the truth."_**

**_The black man has and have become so fucked that we don't even know our roots; true heritage and life story not his – story; what they tell us._**

Sick am I of my own because wi too fool fool an dunkkya.

Wi radda become clown in the devils system instead of investing and creating our own. We radda mash up fi wi and adopt another man's own rather than fix what's broken with us; our own.

Wi radda walk, talk and sleep with the devil rather than let him go.

Man how it gets under my skin how we've become self centered, conceited and egotistical fools walking on the bridge of death.

If we were so educated and knowledgeable humanity would not be in the mess we are in. The black communities globally would not be in a mess. We would be more advanced in a civilized and positive way.

If we were so knowledgeable and civilized, he Good God and Allelujah would be walking hand in hand beside me and you daily literally.

We would not have a need for the false, lying and deceiving governments of the world because he Good God and Allelujah would be our everything.

We would not have a need for the false, lying and deceiving clergies of the world. Come on now. Clergies that send us to hell; death with their lies.

Religion is true death. Hence when the devil's clan came to colonize man – the civilized of other lands including our own, they took religion with them to deceive us (you) and take your land(s); home. They indoctrinated humanity with their god and lies and now look at humanity globally today.

Fighting for a dead god, Aries the god of war – death just for a place in hell. Hence Zeus, Heysuis; your so called Jesus. Go back to Adam and Eve. Satan did Eve hence a form of evil was born. Modern day demons that walk and plague the earth. Demons that use religion to trap and deceive man hence Eve died. She thought she would become a god but she did not become a god did she? She died and went straight to hell because she disobeyed God – Good God. Hence hell is her home until this day literally.

Religion has you believing in God – their God of Death and Destruction. And just like Eve (Evening) you are going to die. Hence the extinction of humanity (Billions) real soon before 2032. Good God gave us all life and we are to live life good and true; clean. Hence the life you live on earth determines where you go in the spiritual realm. Afterlife.

If man was so knowledgeable and civilized, He God – Good God and Allelujah would be all we need. He would be in the mist of all that we do in goodness and in truth daily and or each and every day.

He would be the positive and clean force we have and need in our lives and not death. Come on now.

Wi too damn bright and wrenk hence none, not one of us know God – Good God and Allelujah literally.

Wi damn bare face. Hence no wonder the black race is disconnected from Good God and Allelujah literally. We've lost our spirituality hence we can no longer tell time and stop time – death.

Hence I now ask every black man, woman and child this question; WHERE IS YOUR GOD?

Go on tell me your god is the God of Isaac, Ishmael and Abraham. Tell me your God is Jesus and or Jehovah. Go ahead mek me call unnu cunnumunnu of the highest order and degree; kind. Damn fool. We were taught this including me. Why the hell do I need the God of Isaac, Jacob, Ishmael and Abraham if I already have mine, my own?

What makes their god better than my God; the Black Man's God? Come on now.

*What has the God of Isaac, Jacob, Ishmael and Abraham done for me; you? Are they not Babylonians that has and have raped us of our lands, women, men, riches, children, heritage, language, spirituality and place with Good God long ago? Isn't this the same god that is leading the Black Race straight to hell? So why the hell would I want any of them?*

*Go on and say it, hence I ask again, BLACK MAN WHERE IS YOUR GOD?*

You know the Babylonian System is that of death. But yet you follow them to your deaths and accept their profits (money) sorry prophets. Woops puppets to save us.

Unnu the black race mimic dem an carry on like dem like unnu a Babylon batty literally.

Wey unnu own dey?
Wey fi unnu dey?

But yet many of you are so fucking ignorant that you don't know that your shit stinks like the next man or woman; person. And the book; so called holy bible is watered down crap of your history combined with Hindu (Babylonian) history – stories but yet you hold this book in high esteem. Say it's divinely inspired. How the hell can a book based on incest – family ram business be holy?

Wait a suh Gad nasty fi mek faada an daughta procreate with each other?

Wow.

Gad truly tek di case because yu tun nasty lacka man – humanity to blurnaught. Wow. Man wicked een.

Let me ask you this. How can nastiness be holy?

Our history is nasty – unclean but yet we say it's holy and clean. Hold it (our nasty history) in high esteem.

We do not hold Good God in high esteem but yet we hold self and the nastiness of self in high regard – esteem.

Wow

And we say that nasty and perverted incestual book of family rams clean. Ram Quran and or Ramkoran depending on your spelling. We value nastiness over clean. Hence I ask yet again, Black Man where is your God?

When did the nasty gods of Babylon become ours?

How can we say the bible is clean when all in it is unclean?

When did dirt and stench become our fashion statement (clothing) – way of life?
Come on tell me when?

Unnu go smell unnu self because unnu stink literally. Good God is clean not stink. He does not like stench hence he's left billions of us to our own stench literally.

Look after your own and secure your own idiboo. No wonder the devil favours the black race over all other races because like I've said before, the devil can set im pot pan eee stove and rest assured within a nana second we sell out Good God and Allelujah for him literally.

Listen if Satan was a betting man he would win all the time. No, scrap that. He is a betting man hence he wins over God – Good God and

Allelujah all the time when it comes to man – humanity. All we have to do is take a look at our sins – disgrace that we do daily globally.

He doesn't have to do anything because HIS WEAPON IS JESUS. Hence all of you are his weapons against Good God and Allelujah literally.

He screwed Eve (Evening) by telling her in his book of sin that she would become a GOD if she did what he said. SHE DID AND LOST HER LIFE AND PLACE WITH GOOD GOD AND ALLELUJAH INDEFINITELY and we are no exception today. He has us and smiling brightly too.

Now he's given the lots of you JESUS and all of you have and has lost your place with Good God and Allelujah literally. Don't believe me? Just take a look at the people of this earth fighting for control and what the next man has and have; land and resources. Many are fighting for a dead god that tells them to rob and steal; take what don't belong to them without knowing that their place in the end will be hell. They will be surrounded by fire and consumed by fire for hundreds of thousands of years before they eventually die. Satan himself gave his people religion to deceive you whilst taking your land and colonizing you. Hence truly woe be unto many countries that have done this. Rob and kill people for what rightfully belongs to them (those people). But none should be surprised at this because the book of sin, so called holy bible did advocate theft and death because the god in this book who we call God was before many armies on the battlefield taking life just like his wicked and evil, vile and deceitful people. They killed for a place in hell hence Satan is in hell rotting and or burning right now. We refuse to accept life hence death is accepted globally by man – humanity. I don't want death hence its life – good and positive life over death is what I say.

Some are indefinitely lost to death; hell whilst others are on the border line. A couple more sins and you will be gone indefinitely on the other side – hell.

No Good God I am bent. Many lands were taken by force and what gives anyone the right to do this?

What gives anyone the right to colonize anyone and take what belongs to them?

You raped the land and people. Indoctrinated them in your filth and prisons that you call religion. You took their souls (life) and sent them to hell whilst leaving their land barren and penniless. Then you have the gaul to turn around and say we will help you. All you have to do is borrow this amount of money and oppress your people. Keep them starving and begging while you plunge the knife in their backs a little bit more. You made people give up their place with God – Good God and Allelujah and accept death. Your dead and decaying god and this is wrong. Hence death comes; walk amongst man – humanity literally.

Yes I know many did not listen to you hence we cannot stop selling you out. We can't stop disobeying you. That one lie that Eve (Evening) believed in is still costing us. Instead of learning we refuse to hence truly look at humanity today. Look at the death toll of man – humanity. Hence truly woe be unto man real and very soon.

When are we going to stop falling for the tricks of the devil?

When are we going to start truly trusting Good God and go back to him? Come on now.

Life is worth it. So why do we give up our lives so willingly to death?

What makes death so much better than life? Come on now.

In all I've seen, I've also seen the haves of the black community look down on the have nots.

Many squander and become broke.

Many die of diseases
Drugs
Domestic Violence
Gang Warfare
Biological Warfare (War)

Trust me I've been looked down upon because I do not fit the mold of a civilized black society, money education and power; lies and deceit. I am not a part of the norm that base their lives on religious lies and deceit; political power and wealth. I am the disobedient one because I am neither a field nor am I a house slave that live by the rules and regulations of Massa – the global slave trade.

I am different because I am rebellious; can't be bought and sold.

I live by my own terms hence I am a threat to society, the norms of society globally. No one wants to know the truth but yet everyone is expecting Good God and Allelujah to sacrifice someone to save them.

In all I know, when evil comes, he and she comes with religions of death to kill you and steal your land, home and place with Good God and Allelujah. They bring their false education of their corrupt system to get you to leave your own and worship them, their disgusting filth of a god and gods; god's that have no moral values, class and beauty – truth.

Their god is so stink that he Good God and Allelujah has and have been trying to separate us from them and we are the ones that refuse to listen because the little piece of pork (swine and beef – cow) suits us just fine.

Yes they keep us hungry whilst devising their economic plots filled with their own words that it leaves you homeless, penniless and deprived. They give us their book of filth called the Holy Bible and say this book of nastiness and filth is of Good God and Allelujah holy when they know it is not it is the stench of sin; sin's holy book. This book is of the devil; their god because the wording in this book kill you and send you straight to hell. All that we were not to do we did hence making this book death's book, the book of the dead because all who believe in the god and gods of these book are going directly to hell literally. We've become dead like them hence we walk and talk in all manner of filth just like them. Hence the death; extinction of the devil's clowns – people real soon. The full charcoal black moon is a testament, the winding down of humans globally because they did believe in the dead; gods of the dead. Therefore, humanity globally bowed down to these gods; gods of the dead and now they must pay, must go to hell and die. They raised the dead, sacrificed for the dead hence becoming the children of the dead literally.

Yes I'm looked upon as being poor because of circumstances but who the hell cares as long as Good God and Allelujah truly loves me.

Been told by my own black man that he does not want anyone (date anyone) that do not make the same amount of money as him. For me this is fine because at the end of the day stability and or financial prosperity isn't dependant on the amount of money I make or have in my bank account. It's dependent on the good I do for others, Good God and Allelujah; me. Yes money helps to pay the bills but when my riches come and will come it will be shared amongst Me, Good God and Allelujah, his people and my people including land (Mother Earth) and the economy of the land and my true family. We will build together positively in a positive and true way for us, Hood God and Allelujah, the land and people of the land. And once our lands become prosperous and truly organic truly do not want or need anything from us nor want to vacation in or on our properties. There will be no sharing with you because I am truly expecting Good God and Allelujah including Earth to separate us in goodness and in truth from all of you infinitely and indefinitely forever ever without end.

Hence I ask Blackman where is your God because obviously you have none?

Damn from a race of educated and rich people to a bunch of clowns that have sold their souls to the devil for a little bickle (food) and a place in hell with him the devil.

Many of us are left so poor by our own that mothers turn daughters into prostitutes just to get a little food.

Young boys prostitute themselves for a little food – shilling; shelter.

Education, education, the system is plagued by disaster that adequate books cannot be found – go around.

Black lands have become so poor and destitute not even our own care for our own literally.

None want to live in Africa.

None want to go back home.

The West is the best to some. But little do they know of the trap and traps of the West. We build the West whilst our home, Africa lay in ruin; poverty and disrepair.

We build the West whilst our home, Africa is plagued by drought, disease, war, pestilence including human pestilence and inadequate funding to fund their own amongst other things. We became lost, no not lost in this case. We became caught in the system, rat race as Bob Marley said. A System and Rat Race that say this can be yours if you play my game; follow my rules; become clowns.

Ah yes we got caught up in the lies.

The promise of everything including fame, money; the blame game. But instead of being truthful to self and our God we became sacrificial lambs. Lambs that slaughtered self, deceived self and became a part of the living breathing and walking dead; hell.

We sacrificed it all for a place in hell.

Many cannot go back home because the leaders; governments and people (army) of the land made sure there's no land; home to go back to.

People fighting against the army and the army fighting against the people. Now beheading is the norm in many lands including my own.

*Citizens are not safe because the house of the dead, your Parliament, Senate, Churches, NATO and IMF made sure of this. In all they did, they sacrificed you, all of you in humanity to the devil; hell. As nations we are not united and never will be united in truth. You are all united in the cause of death; the devil's cause (NATO). War is never the answer to war nor can anyone go on the battlefield of death with Aries and win. You will end up losing lives, land, economy – your own soul and place with Good God and Allelujah literally. So to say you are NATO and have a united front is just a front for the DEVIL'S CAUSE LITERALLY. YOU TAKE PEOPLE – HUMAN LIVES TO HELL LITERALLY BECAUSE YOU CANNOT TAKE EARTH. THE EARTH DOES NOT BELONG TO ANY OF YOU AND NEVER WILL. HENCE YOU STEAL LANDS AND LEAVE THE NATIVES OF THE LAND IMPOVERISHED POOR AND WANTING, WANTING OF FOOD, WATER, SHELTER; THEIR OWN SPIRITUALITY. You stole their God and pollute their land with your own decrepit and decaying own. In all everyone of you do, you sacrifice your own and others to death. You developed your monetary front called the IMF to rape and rob lands including people of their wealth and dignity. You dictate to nations because you leave them constantly borrowing from you; drained financially whilst imposing unfair trade practices so that these nations never rise economically; spiritually. You let these government tax the poor severely hence people rising up, going to war and taking arms (fight) against their own. You create death because you're all loan sharks and extortionists of the worst and highest kind. You're not rebels but terrorists that walk around and rob lands of their life and economic stability. Yes you think you are wise in all that you do to rape and kill people, but in all honesty, the DEVIL IS WISER THAN THE LOTS OF YOU BECAUSE HE HAS ALL OF YOU LOCKED IN HELL LITERALLY. YOUR CONTAINMENT UNIT IN HELL AWAITS THE LOTS OF YOU HENCE EVERY NATION THAT IS UNDER THE NATO AND IMF BANNER GOOD GOD HAS AND HAVE A BONE TO PICK WITH THE LOTS OF YOU LITERALLY. Death is your game and play, hence you're all dead – a part of the walking and living dead literally.*

Instead of helping the people and nations globally you pit nations against nations by creating war whilst telling them you are keeping them alive. Now I ask you this, how is war keeping the next man alive?

How is war and strife helping the next man's land and people?

Yes nations and people have and has become victims of the Oppressed. Men and women like you; you that say they have control – are that powerful, the all powerful. You sit in high chairs playing god.

Selecting and refusing.

Controlling and manipulating whilst leaving nations and people needy – hungry and depraved. But shortly all that you do to manipulate, control and kill must come to an end.

*NATO MUST CRUMBLE FOR ALL THE WRONGS AND EVIL IT HAS DONE GLOBALLY FOR DECADES.*

The IMF will need and seek bailout shortly BCAUSE ALL THEY DO TO HURT AND HUMILIATE LANDS, KEEP PEOPLE AND COUNTRY WANTING, NEEDY AND STARVING; HUNGRY ***MUST RETURN TO THEM.*** All they did and still do to rape hurt and control Black Lands globally they must pay – collapse indefinitely forever ever without end. Wickedness and greed, dishonesty, extortion and evil was your will from the get go. So all that has joined forces with you, must pay and will pay – come to an indefinite and forever ever end. All families and or family members that are associated with all of you must join all of you in hell literally. Thus saith the Lord thy God meaning it is so. You do not hurt others and leave them wanting and fighting; killing without consequences. You do not leave people hungry and needy. You do not kill because the law plainly and specifically say, "thou shalt not kill, thou shalt not steal," amongst others.

Murder is murder because murder is death, death of all physically and spiritually. And not because you kill does not mean you will not have to pay for your sins. You have to pay for them, hence death is time; in time at a point in time. Death does not normally come right away for some. It takes time to come and when it does come it takes all depending on the severity of your sins and the magnitude of sins that are racked up by the people of or in your land. When we sin, death is guaranteed hence sin not and death will not come. Cannot come. If we sin not then death will have nothing to do. Hence death dies; must die because there is nothing for him and her to do; take.

You took life and killed millions' hundreds of millions in the process and because of this all must be taken from you including your land. The land and lands you set up shop in. You never thought of life and how sacred and blessed true life is. So because of this no forgiveness, penance and repentance must be given to any of you including your families. You took away from life – Good God and Allelujah; the Breath of Life. So as you take from the Breath of Life all must truly be taken from all of you. You are guaranteed a forever ever place with death in hell because death is whom you killed for; serve as well as protect. (Police). You had no regard for life so unto hell you must go indefinitely without end until your final death comes. Thus saith the Lord because thy will is done in hell and unto hell you must now go meaning it is so. Your hell is thy own because you created it indefinitely with the wrongs you have done and the unfair laws that you made to hurt man – others and land; country – humanity.

Ah what a day when the bell tolls for all of you because hell truly awaits you; the leaders and people of debt and death; NATO AND THE IMF INCLUDING POLITICAL LEADERS AND CHURCH LEADERS GLOBALLY.

Ah yes from queens and kings we came
We developed
Created; paved the way. But over time we found fault in our own.
Found fault in our own God
Creation (s)

We wanted that which was not ours

We praised the deities and gods of others
Denounced and renounced our own

We found him redundant amongst other things.

Said we didn't care. Told him the offerings of the
devil was more lucrative and precious than his.
Instead of keeping our own we gave him up for
nothing – a false god.

False hope
False everything
A place in hell literally.

We left ourselves naked
Penniless
Hungry
Destitute
Illiterate
Without an identity, roots – our true history.
Heritage
Home
Culture

We made our children go hungry whilst they
took our land
They cast us out
Became cast out

They classed us as slaves
Made us slaves

Slave owned

They called us monkeys
Niggers
Coons
Baboons
Buffoons
Darkies
The curse; people of the cursed

All that we were that was excellent, righteous, good and clean; we had to give up and did give up to accept lands, countries, people, languages, hair, clothes, religion and food that was truly not our own.

We became the outcast because our god did not want us again anymore. We faced difficulties, hardships, pain, sufferings including death. We faced it all and still we could not return; learn. We refuse to listen, take heed. It was no different then and it's still no different now. We know about Noah's Ark and who were saved, but because of a promise of that sacrificial lamb (Jesus) billions believe in him that they will be saved. ***BUT HOW QUICKLY HUMANITY HAS FORGOTTEN ABOUT THE LIE THAT WAS TOLD TO EVE (EVENING). HOW QUICKLY THAT THEY FORGOT THAT SHE DID DIE AND DID NOT LIVE.***

## SHE WENT AGAINST GOOD GOD AND ALLELUJAH AND DIED ALL AROUND. HENCE I ASK YET AGAIN, IF THE LIE DID NOT WORK FOR EVE, HOW IS THE JESUS LIE GOING TO HELP YOU AND SAVE YOU; WORK FOR YOU?

*One lie down (Eve), the second one we are living in this day and time (Jesus). Virtually everyone globally believes in Jesus, the Jesus lie. And now it's up to us (the children of Good God and Allelujah) to not make it a third one. We must separate ourselves from the guilty, those who have been charged and found guilty of sin without knowing. Billions have been found guilty hence the true Jews (children and people) of Good God and Allelujah MUST TAKE SHELTER FROM THE STORM. THE HARVEST (STORM AND STORMS OF DEATH COMES BEFORE 2032) AND WE HAVE TO SECURE SELF AND NOT GET CAUGHT UP IN IT LEST WE DIE WITH THEM – THE CHILDREN OF THE WICKED AND DECEITFUL – EVIL.*

*We had one extinction (Noah and his time). The second is yet to come before 2032.*

*The third one I am hoping Good God and Allelujah will stay infinitely and indefinitely forever ever without end after all is said and done before 2032.*

*2132 is no more so let's hope and pray death stays dead in hell for all infinity indefinitely never to ever rise on Earth or in the kingdoms and abode of Good God and his people forever ever indefinitely for more than indefinite infinities.*

The pain our ancestors felt was unbearable and inhumane. They were taken from our lands and beautiful homes as slaves to become slave owned – the servants of men (Abdullah) – the uncivilized and uncultured; the uneducated and illiterate.

We were taught our beautiful black skin is ugly but yet they steal our history and identity including our god and say it is theirs. They do all to look like us and be like us. They even took our men and women; children too. For some our children are their fashion statement because it's cool to have little black babies; Nigger Babies to comfort their own shame, selfish pride; guilt and inhumane treatment.

*Some say, "Look I have a Nigger Baby hence I am one of you. I adopted him her because Mama couldn't afford her him. I am doing a good thing, I'm not racist. See I have your son, daughter."* But a pity many do not know

BLACKMAN REDEMPTION – BLACKMAN WHERE IS YOUR GOD?

adoption is a another form of slavery because you buy people's babies, hence the exchange of money. Money is paid for human life – babies. Hence the global slave and sex trade still exist for the wealthy. Yes blood money on a global scale. You are all guilty and without shame and morals because people, in this case children are bought and sold globally.

*Yes they took our way of communication, now we can no longer communicate with Good God. We can no longer go home because we are locked out, truly locked out of God's – Good God and Allelujah's kingdom and abode.*

**What a shame because we no longer know where home is.**

Yes, we've lost it all but we cannot blame others we have to blame self. We did not respect ours nor did we respect and truly love our own god; what he Good God and Allelujah has and have given us.

Our drumbeat became tainted because we no longer have rhythm. Hence we can no longer feel our spiritual beat; heartbeat.

We can no longer communicate though sound and vibration.
Touch

Smell
Feel

***Many have and has lost it all. Hence Mother, Mother Africa no longer knows her own. Nor does she care for her own. Sad yes but this is our reality. The reality of a race that gave up all to death and for death. We played the game and lost. We let the devil in and the devil took it all including our lives.***

Mother Africa we call, cry out.

Mother Africa we want to come home we sing, preach and talk.

Mother Africa we're not lost we are still here we plea.

But in all our pleas and cries, we could not find her; still can't find her.

We lost it all and her doors are almost closed to us all.

In all we did, we lost her identity and our identity

We lost our way of life
Worship
Children
True home
True life

We are no longer Africans because Africa is no longer in us. We cannot hear her heartbeat, hear her cry.

Cannot feel the vibe
The vibrations of her drums
The soul in her speech
Cry
Life.

We left her and now we are dying at a massive rate in lands that are truly not our own. Foreign lands we call home.

We are mistreated
Lied to
Abused
Killed
Young men and women no longer respect their queens
Kings
Self

We've become valueless

Devalued like the global currencies of different lands

Young women are no longer a part of the pack; pact. They've lost their pride, have no pride in self, shame, ambition; self respect.

We've become lowly
Drugged out
Sexed out

Shacked and Chained by a system that have no remorse and moral values. A system that cares not for its own.

We sell sex
Whatever we can to get another fix.

We sell music; tainted music; crime (Rap and Dancehall).

We are no longer children of God- Good God
We are no longer clean
Truthful

We've become children of whores because on any given day you can find us on the street corner prostituting ourselves, even selling blow to the highest bidder. Yes that record contract, shoe deal, any contract for that matter including

Weed, the Mary Jane's, Bob Marley's, Poppers and Molly's.

Yes money have and has to be made and you just got to get paid – laid.

Pity because you are worth nothing, not even a dime on a global scale.

*TOO BLACK*
*NOT PRETTY ENOUGH*
*HAIR TOO NAPPY, COARSE*

*Too fat*
*Too skinny*

*You're too fly*
*Ghetto*
*Poor*

Ah, chi ching ching you just got laid and paid because the dollar bill is all over you. Hence you gave your lap dance and the loose change given was just another part of the deal; yours.

Money, money, money just take a look at some of your kids.

Spoilt brats that know not charity; the value and true meaning of giving.

Yes we are paid slaves that work for the system. Like I said, we got laid and paid. Yes and hence the poll dance and lap dance was fine and now you have to continue doing it, bow, bow down low if you know what I mean.

Don't go there because it's in the contract hence the Black Skin and Black Man is worth nothing. Not a damned thing a part from the little chump change that is given to some.

Let's do the monkey dance. Better yet let them go from tree to tree. But with all that said and done, Mama Africa is still being raped by you and me.

All is taken from her but as so called Africans that have faced turmoil in other people's wicked and evil lands, we cannot give a helping hand to the Mother and Place that gave birth to us; all of humanity – our true ancestors. We cannot honour her hence we suffer in lands that are truly not our own. We also make her (Mother Africa) suffer because all we can do is talk about her goodness; her – the land we use to call home.

All we talk about is us being taken from her (Africa) as slaves.

All we can talk about is the Mother Land but when it truly comes to helping her (the Mother Land) and honouring her as we would our mother and father; Good God and Allelujah, we cannot do this for her or to her in her.

We would rather watch her being raped and taken advantage of.

We would rather watch others strip her naked of all her dignity and put our ancestors in turmoil rather than truly help her; invest in her.

We would rather continue to be Massa's clowns, slaves, buffoons; fools rather than return home and truly help our own.

We would rather stay stumbling – falling rather than rise up in truth, true peace and harmony rather than return home and build home.

Like I said, all we have is talk. But in truth we truly do not care because we allow others to rape her (Mother Africa) and her people of all including resources, spiritual and ethical life. (True Ether).

We say Africa and African, but neither Africa and African is within us. We do not build her, cannot build her because SHE IS TRULY NOT OUR OWN. We know not Africa nor do we truly know what it means nor do we know what it's like to be from MOTHER, THE MOTHER LAND – AFRICA. AFRICA IS OUR COUNTRY, LAND, HERITAGE AND LIFE. AFRICA IS BLACK COUNTRY – THE KINGDOM THAT STARTED IT ALL. SHE GAVE BIRTH TO TRUE AND GOOD LIFE – ALL.

Now we suffer like little children; disobedient children because Mama has and have become unknown to us; me and you.

We are disconnected from her because billions of us are not born in her. Do not know her; the birth place of all human and spiritual life.

She is the center of the universe
The hub of all life

She is the giver and beginning of all life.
She will never end because there are no endings to life, just beginnings. Beginnings that grow up and glow.

As Africans we cannot wake up.

We refuse to build positively.

We refuse to stand up in unity positively.

We refuse to go back to the birthplace and womb of life; Mama – Mama Africa.

So we continue to build in lands that are not our own.

We continue to sell out Mama.
Rape her of her children
Me and You.

We continue to neglect her; abuse her, rape and kill her children.

Mama is the cradle of life SO RETURN MY PEOPLE AND TRULY BUILD HER POSITIVELY. SHE IS THE TRUE ARK OF THE COVENANT HENCE TRUE LIFE CAME FROM HER; BEGAN THERE. No land and continent can lay claim to life but Mama can; Mother Africa can.

We've become ungrateful
Selfish
Self absorbed because in all we say, we've truly done nothing positive to help Mama – Mama Africa; Her.

We would rather talk and spend our wealth on and in other lands rather than truly flock to her and vacation in her. On her property – our own.

We would rather build others rather than build her for the future – a better way - tomorrow.

## *Africa is a part of God. She is of him – the female version of him hence life centers around her and she is the TRUE HEART OF THINGS.*

True life came from her but in all that we do; we cannot treat her properly; respect her and truly love her. As we do to Good God and Allelujah we do to her and unto her, hence mans loyalty is not with Good God and Earth, all that sustains and maintains us; God and Mother Earth.

We would rather give other lands our blessings rather than share with her, let her become blessed once again.

We would rather spend in Babylon and give Babylon all instead of investing in Mama – Mama Africa. Kenya, Sudan (Sud – South of the Garden where true life began), Somalia, Uganda, South Africa, Lesotho and Swaziland to name a few. These lands are calling. Won't we vacation there?

Can't we go there; home?

Can't we help our brothers and sisters with a home; a true home?

Can't we help our brothers and sisters with school supplies, food, clothing, a television; MEDICAL SUPPLIES, shoes, a rose bud or even a flower?

Can't we sing glory to the behold and respect Mama – Mother Africa?

Can't we give back that little to make Mama, Mama Africa hold her head up high and say my children thank you I am filled with pride? Now come home because my door is now truly open unto to you. Do not do as your ancestors did. Do not sell out your own but respect your own and do good and well to your own including me. Keep me close and dear to your hearts.

Let me shine in prosperity and beauty once again so that I can truly bless you forever ever without end.

Put down violence and strife, war and hate because all these things truly hurt me; are not of me. Let me help you to live in true harmony harmoniously so that you can grow up to see my husband; my other half, Good God and Allelujah himself.

Instead of truly loving Mama we return hate unto her.

We desecrate our skins (tattoos) instead of returning to her whole and true.

Instead of keeping our blessings we take our blessings and give it to other land and lands instead of truly blessing Mama with truth, true love and prosperity. We do not keep or help Mama, Mama Africa with our blessings. We do not share with her but yet we say we are of African descent; our ancestors came from her – Africa.

Many of our ancestors were sold by our own yes. But instead of learning and returning home and say you bought our ancestors, sold them to the highest bidder. You took away their rights to life including dignity now I am doing this.

*I am going home, coming home to build my own and honour my ancestors, my mothers and fathers so that they too can live and rise up in goodness and in truth to Good God and Allelujah forever ever indefinitely.*

*Instead of doing this, we do not do a damned thing. We would rather wallow like pigs in their jails whilst begging for a damned hand out.*

*We would rather die at the hands of our oppressor rather than secure a place for ourselves home.*

*We would rather beg our oppressors for change – a little dung rather than take our good knowledge and experience and return to Africa – Mama Africa and build her in a positive and good way indefinitely.*

*IN ALL WE DO, WE DO NOT TRULY THINK OF HER.*

*WE DO NOT SEE AFRICA, BUT YET WE SAY WE ARE DESCENDENTS OF AFRICANS.*

*WE DO NOT KNOW HER NOR DO WE KNOW HER LANGUAGES, BUT YET WE SAY WE CAN CALL AFRICA HOME.*

*We refuse positive unity.*

*We refuse to truly help her; our own hence, I ask you yet again.*

*BLACK MAN WHERE IS YOUR GOD AND CREATOR; GOOD GOD AND ALLELUJAH?*

Many have and has sold their souls to be a part of the devil's society.
Many kill to eat

Many ignore their own
Show off on their own

Many die in lands they can't call home.

Many say they are of Africa but cannot lend a true and helping hand to Africa.

Many can't find Africa because to them (many) Africa is but a continent. But a pity they do not know that Africa gave birth to all the lands of the earth.

Pity they do not know that Africa is the whole entire universe.

We buy big house and throw away money. We buy prostitutes and whores, side chicks but when it comes to Africa and our African people, we cannot build or buy a home to put one; our own.

We cannot buy food to feed one like I've said. Some even refuse to buy one a pair of shoes but yet we say we are African this and African that. We spend so much on the American dream but yet forget about our African home and well being; ancestry – dream and dreams.

We dare to dream about Africa because Africa is not on our radar.

*We class ourselves as African American, Afro Canadian, Afro Caribbean; you name it we say it, but when it comes to our African HOME, HERITAGE AND ROOTS INCLUDING AFRICAN HAIR; WE NEGLECT IT AND CARE FOR ANOTHER MAN'S OWN. We buy fake this and that whilst forgetting realness and real everything of Africa.*

*We forget the real and nappy hair.*
*Big butts, short and natural long hair.*
*Round firm breasts; that fine ass, lovely piece of waist.*

*Ah yes the beautiful black skin and more than sexy everything that radiates in the sun; moonlight.*

*Skin more delicate than a rose that's frozen in time, is time.*

*Skin that's finer than wine; perfectly cooked; done.*

*Damn he she is so good to eat; better than any meat.*

*He She is my vegetables*
*My healing everything*
*Play thing*
*Sexual healing*

*Sexual everything*

*Yes the magnificence of her him*
*Eye catching*
*More than appealing*
*Baby divine*
*Divinity*
*My everything. Damn baby you are fine.*
*Mine*

*Wow, the Black Man Woman is fine*
*Damned fine*
*Heavenly*

*Ah yes, lineage of Kings*
*Queens*
*Scent more beautiful than Kush*
*Frankensense and Myrrh*
*Opium*

*Ah people, people, my beautiful Black People*
*Jaw dropping*
*Eye popping*

*The envy of all the universe; everything.*

We say we are African and Proud, but yet Africa lay in ruin; poor. We would rather let others rape Africa and treat the people and children worse than second class citizens – dogs; than do something to help our own. We let others rape us of our African Pride; All but yet we pree Africa and all that is African.

How can this be?

*Hence we are pitied; poor.*
*Pity the poor, pity di poor.*

*Pity the blind because we are blind.*

*Pity the (di) poor, AFRICANS CAN'T AFFORD ANYTHING NOT EVEN THEIR OWN. THEY CAN'T AFFORD MEDICATION SO WE HAVE TO SAVE THEM. GIVE THEM OUR WHAT NOT AND WHAT LEF. THE THINGS WE DON'T WANT.*

*GIVE TO THE POOR AND DESTITUE; AFRICA. THEY CAN'T AFFORD ANYTHING BECAUSE BLACK PEOPLE ONLY HAVE BABIES THAT THEY CAN'T*

*AFFORD. THEY ARE OUR BURDEN; WHAT WE DON'T WANT TO BE LIKE IN SOCIETY. ALL THEY DO IS HAVE CHILDREN THAT BECOME SLAVES.*

*Children that sit at the road corner drinking and selling drugs.*

*They are uneducated*
*Bums*

*They are vicious*
*Gang bangers; members.*

*LOOK AT THEM, SLAVES OF A DIFFERENT KIND. HENCE WE'VE BECOME THE SHAMED AND SHAMELESS THAT HAS AND HAVE BEEN LEFT FOR DEAD BY EVERYONE IN THE GLOBAL SOCIETY.*

*This is our sad reality and it is truly a shame.*

*Yes some hide under foundations and lie about what they do for Africa and Africans. All they collect, only a fraction goes to towards Africa and Africans if any goes to them at all. Africa has become the go to place hence we've become beggars and street people begging for a handout.*

*We've become homeless*
*Hopeless*
*Thoughtless*
*Have nots*

**Trust, we have not because in all that we do, many still cannot go to or go back to Africa to build their ancestral home.**

Many are stuck here wondering what it would be like to walk home. Return to the Womb of Life – Mother Africa, the Mother Land. Hence we are truly pitied and left for dead.

There is so much to life but we cannot accept life because life has left many of us at the wayside. The reality of life we do not know because life isn't real to many of us anymore. Too much hardships and pain.

Too much depression, psychological issues an unstable brain.

Medications, medications, there's a few. Hence you find many blacks on the psychotic and coo coo train.

You find many of us drug induced
Drugged out
Suicidal
Bleached out and shelled out
Without knowledge of self.

We do not build our own. We take up the nastiness of other cultures and say we belong when we truly do not; say it's our own. Then when we go insane we cry out in pain; blame the devil for our lack or morals, truth and values.

We look down on our own skin.
Self
True Black Pride
Race

We would rather walk in the valley of the shadow of death and die instead of bypassing death's valley and walk in and on the valley of truth.

Yes we are a mess. Have become the mess and messes of society.

We say we want better but refuse to do better. So we march and protest our unfair and unjust treatment; the death of the old and young.

Death of children
You

No there are no reviews because the Black Man is low on the Pagan Totem Pole. Hence we have no true stars. No African Walk of Fame.

No African Hall of Fame
No African Science (hair)
No African Museums
No African Anything.

We've forgotten where we came from hence many refuse to leave these unfair and unjust lands and go back home. It seems the hardship, abuse, pain and sufferings suits us fine. Hence we refuse to give up Babylon and leave Babylon and return home.

It seems the name calling and labeling suits us just fine.

It seems the killing and beheading of our children suits us.

The raping of young children and women suits us just fine.

It seems the drug abuse and mental instability suits us.

The prison terms of shame suits us just fine.

It seems the lack of housing and money; ghettos suit us just fine.

The diseases, immorality; lack of family and family values suits us just fine.

Hence we have no roots to call our own anymore. Our tree of life is lost; have become lost to many.

Dead

Instability is what we want; hence the jail houses of hell (physical hell) houses so many of us; our own.

Young men and women have and has become caught up in the system, Political and Penal Systems, Spiritual Prisons; Medical and Financial Systems. Systems that weren't meant to help us but meant to enslave and kill us. Now look at it; a race war is inevitable because Babylon (the Police Force) globally has and have targeted our young men and women including old. The killing spree has begun because it is being instigated and we (the black men and women including children of society) are the preys. If only we had listened long ago then we would not be in this mess. But instead of coming out of the mess and build a good and true society for our own, we stay in the mess and wallow like pigs in pig sty and wonder why the Black Man and Race can't be any better. Why we can't prosper; have our true own.

We sell ourselves short whilst playing the clowns – fools in a system that was not designed for us but designed and meant to kill us. Go back into history. We became captured souls that were indoctrinated and conditioned (classical conditioning) in Paganism – Religion and Religious Dung. They gave us a god that was not ours nor even come close to ours. But yet we refuse to see this and walk away from the devil's own. Everywhere the devil went he took religion with him. Hence enslaving, ridiculing and calling others uncivilized when they were and still are the true uncivilized ones. In all they do, they kill and steal, rape to have what you have; destroy. They knew (the devil and his wicked and evil people) could not take us, hence they made weapons and diseases to kill us whilst stealing our riches, richness and blessings of life.

*Everywhere the devil and his people went they took guns (weapons) – war and strife with them. They knew religion is a lie so they sold you on this lie and you could not see that what they were doing was selling you false hope whilst leaving you penniless – had; physically and spiritually dead.*

*They kept you hence you became their whores that would kill to eat, wallow in dung; kill your own for them. Peace was never in their hearts hence they were Men of War, men that killed and took your own.*

*In all we did we accepted the devil and his own including books of dung – lies that cheated you out of your soul, life; everything.*

*Many of us refuse to listen and still refuse to listen. Hence many did not care to learn. So we became displaced and disgraced; the used and abused.*

Many of us know not where in the womb and cradle of life we originate. (Africa)

Yes it's disheartening, but we were the ones to forget about Mother – Mother Africa.

We were the ones that could not and cannot walk away from lands that treat us poorly; worse than slaves.

We are the ones to refuse to allow people to look down on us. Hence we've become slaves of a different and same sort all around.

***We refuse to listen and take pride in ourselves, history, culture, language, home. So we will forever get beatings; be displaced and confused.***

We refuse good for self. Hence we have not our own God because we're slave owned; owned by other gods – deities; slaves.

***We refuse our own god. Hence the beatings will never stop. Death will always come if we continue to refuse to listen. (Adam and Eve)***

Death comes now on a massive scale, hence I ask yet again, Black Man where is your God?

Who is going to save you when the harvest comes?

What land and or lands are you going to run to when the Babylonian System globally collapse?

Africa, Mama Africa is there so you had better find your little piece of land – true home.

We have to return, hence the diseases they create and spread; the propaganda they spread in the Mother Land so that we cannot return home.

They want us to stay their slaves, but Mama, your true home is calling you so truly return.

Mama is calling you now go home and build her prosperously. No matter the language barrier, learn and truly listen to what he Good God and Allelujah is telling you.

Your spirituality is not totally lost, so go back to being spiritual beings and the universe will open up to you prosperously once again.

They taught us their lies and we learned them. It's now up to us to break free from these lies and build Africa – Mother Africa positively; prosperously. ***We can no longer be a race and people of the separated. We have to unify in truth because "TRUTH IS EVERLASTING LIFE." We have to become the race and people of the united and glorified; blessed. Evil we are to separated from but good and good people cannot separate from each other.***

We have the truth hence we have to live it and live come on now.

We have to put down the lies and corruption of Babylon if we want to live. We know the threat of Babylon and we can no longer continue to give Babylon the victory over us, Good God and Allelujah; THE MOTHER LAND.

Africa is ours so why are we killing Africa?

Why are we allowing others to rape and kill her? She's ours. Now we have to prove that we want her and truly do better for her, self and people.

Pass over Death and leave death and his children alone. Truly build your own. You can do it and you truly know how.

Put down greed. Live for today clean and truthful and tomorrow will bless you in return.

You are not slaves (Pagan) owned. You are Good God's children, so return to the womb and let the cradle of life (Mother Africa) protect and nurture you the right and proper way.

Live clean and be clean and Mama will return all that is good and true, clean and positive unto you.

We must now leave the West and the Devil's people and children to their deaths. They are not our people and will never be our people. Do not miss the Ark of Life because Good God is truly calling you.

HENCE I ASK AGAIN: BLACK MAN WHERE IS YOUR GOD?

Where is your God black man?

What does he look like?

Where did he come from?

## *WHERE ARE YOU GOING IF YOU KNOW NOT YOUR OWN ROOTS?*

Wow, what a life because the black race have and has forgotten where they came from. We've forgotten Mama, the land of our birth – our birthright. We can no longer continue to let Jacob and his people including the god and gods steal and or rob us of our birthright. (Jacob and Esau)

We've forgotten the center and cradle of life, the hub of life – All Life; Mama, Mama Africa. Africa is the land of the Black Man and Woman – Child because true life gave birth in Africa and true life belongs to us all.

Africa is the land of our forefathers and mothers. No, not all of us can claim African Roots and or

African descent but Africa is still our land because of good and true life. Good and true life that was born there as well as came from there.

Africa is in our blood. It is our blood – true right.

***Life was born in Mama hence SHE'S HEART SHAPED – THE HEART OF EVERYTHING GOOD AND TRUE.***

Michelle Jean

*As I close this book I wanted to add my thoughts but I am going to leave things as is. Also note, the picture above I do not own. In writing these books, I am drawn to add pictures and or photos to some but not all of these books. So truly support the artists of the pictures that are in some of these books. These pictures do reflex us and our true beauty including lineage and culture; heritage.*

*There is more to life but that more life is up to you, how you live it. Throughout history we've been brainwashed and manipulated into thinking everything in life is going to be okay when we of our self know that it isn't.*

## We've been brainwashed by religion and religious beliefs; the god figure and this is wrong. Don't get me wrong there is a god, but he's not the god of religion nor is he your Jesus – Zeus.

*God – Good God is with us hence we are to respect life and live life good and clean. We are to enjoy life and live peacefully with our own including others.*

*(Vague I know)*

*As for the black race, you can no longer neglect you and your true history; roots. We know Good God is our root and roots but yet we let him go to becomes slaves and servants in systems that are not our own. Know this. Nothing can be taught to us (the Black Race) because we taught everyone everything. Hence the guardians of the world and universe; universes are predominantly Black and Female. And yes you have Whites and Chinese but Whites you rarely see and or seen.*

*As Blacks we can no longer be gullible fools that pitch tents in foreign lands, lands that hate us; abuse us and kill us.*

*We have our own and that own is Africa. Africa means life; the land of Good God's People.*

**Africa is BLACK LAND hence it is referred to a Nubia; Nubian Land; the land of the Black People. We are Good God's People hence BLACK, THE BANNER OF BLACK WHICH ALL GOOD GOD'S PEOPLE FALL UNDER.**

## ***BLACK IS LIFE BECAUSE HE GOOD GOD AND ALLELUJAH IS BLACK; FALL UNDER THE BANNER OF BLACK AND NOT HUE.***

*Michelle*

# OTHER BOOKS BY MICHELLE JEAN

*Blackman Redemption – The Fall of Michelle Jean*
*Blackman Redemption – After the Fall Apology*
*Blackman Redemption – World Cry – Christine Lewis*
*Blackman Redemption*
*Blackman Redemption – The Rise and Fall of Jamaica*
*Blackman Redemption – The War of Israel*
*Blackman Redemption – The Way I Speak to God*
*Blackman Redemption – A Little Talk With Man*
*Blackman Redemption – The Den of Thieves*
*Blackman Redemption – The Death of Jamaica*
*Blackman Redemption – Happy Mother's Day*
*Blackman Redemption – The Death of Faith*
*Blackman Redemption – The War of Religion*
*Blackman Redemption – The Death of Russia*
*Blackman Redemption – The Truth*
*Blackman Redemption – Spiritual War*
*Blackman Redemption – The Youths*

*The New Book of Life*
*The New Book of Life – A Cry For The Children*
*The New Book of Life – Judgement*
*The New Book of Life – Love Bound*
*The New Book of Life – Me*
*The New Book of Life – Life*

*Just One of Those Days*
*Book Two – Just One of Those Days*
*Just One of Those Days – Book Three The Way I Feel*
*Just One of Those Days – Book Four*

*The Days I Am Weak*
*Crazy Thoughts – My Book of Sin*
*Broken*
*Ode to Mr. Dean Fraser*

*A Little Little Talk*
*A Little Little Talk – Book Two*

*Prayers*
*My Collective*
*A Little Talk/A Time For Fun and Play*
*Simple Poems*
*Behind The Scars*
*Songs of Praise And Love*

*Love Bound*
*Love Bound – Book Two*

*Dedication Unto My Kids*
*More Talk*
*Saving America From A Woman's Perspective*
*My Collective the Other Side of Me*
*My Collective the Dark Side of Me*
*A Blessed Day*
*Lose To Win*
*My Doubtful Days – Book One*

*My Little Talk With God*
*My Little Talk With God – Book Two*

*A Different Mood and World – Thinking*

*My Nagging Day*
*My Nagging Day – Book Two*

*Friday September 13, 2013*
*My True Love*
*It Would Be You*
*My Day*

*A Little Advice – Talk*
*1313, 2032, 2132 – The End of Man*

*Tata*

*MICHELLE'S BOOK BLOG – BOOKS 1 – 18*

*My Problem Day*
*A Better Way*
*Stay – Adultery and the Weight of Sin – Cleanliness Message*

*Let's Talk*
*Lonely Days – Foundation*
*A Little Talk With Jamaica – As Long As I Live*
*Instructions For Death*